What Happens After the Sale

Insights into the Business and Personal

Journey after the big event

By Steve Brody

What Happens After the Sale

Insights into the Business and Personal

Journey after the big event

First published December 2015 by

Brody & Associates
www.brodyassociates.net

ISBN 978   1519 6986 12

Contents

Acknowledgements

This book was prepared as a case study. It will be helpful to many firms who by the forecasts of experts, will be changing hands and going through something similar in the next several years. As such, I want to thank all the CEO Vistage members and Coaching clients that I have been privileged to have as clients. They have shared with me their confidential steps and activities that have led to the transitions talked about here. In particular, the respect that Patrick and his wife, Ann have shared has been critical. This of course, has been the story of the sale of Patrick's firm and the progressing steps that have occurred after. Each step comes with it a specific set of learning and insights.

Tim Levy has provided innovation and creativity when it comes to the publishing of a book. As a Vistage speaker, resource, advisor, consultant and author himself Tim has shown me how to publish a book very rapidly, efficiently, and economically. This has been with the use of outsourcing on a global basis with some talented people who choose to spend some of their time this way. One of those resources has been Sally Odgers, an Australian based editor and author who has helped me on an expedited basis for this book.

In terms of support, I want to thank my loving wife, Sylvia. She has heard many of these stories over and over again and encouraged me to pursue this approach to getting the word out.

Finally, I want to thank those who I have not yet helped create their story. I have described the whole process to help create Patrick's story and the message. They have already asked me to help them create or discover their story. So I look forward to these future projects.

Introduction

Everything is for Sale!

This is the story of the sale of Steel Inc, as related to Steven Brody. The elements described here will apply to many owners of privately held firms. Steel Inc was a firm operating in the Industrial segment of the Oil and Gas business in Texas. The product was specialty steel that was sold to many Oil and Gas firms. It was owned by Patrick and his business partner Simon. Through chapters one to six Patrick tells his story, with additional chapters seven and eight told by Patrick's wife Ann and by me, Steve Brody.

This is a true story, but various names of individuals and the companies involved have been changed.

Chapter One: The Decision to Sell

Background to a Sale

There's a background to any sale. There is a seller (in this case my partner Simon and I) and a buyer (in this case P.S. Forte). This is the sale at its most basic, but when selling a company as a going concern, all sorts of things have to line up for the deal to go ahead satisfactorily for both sides. Here, then, is the situation with my business Steel Inc.

In 2008 Steel Inc had been running for twenty-two years. We were very profitable, and had continued growth each year. We had no debt. It was at that point we were approached by P.S. Forte, which is a publicly-traded company out of Denver, and asked if we had any interest in selling. Some entrepreneurs get tied up in the mindset that *This is my baby. I'll never sell it.* I am different. For me, everything I've got is for sale, except for Ann, my wife. For the right price, I think anything is for sale. We started some discussions with the prospective buyer, and then the financial crisis hit. We were well-prepared and had no problems going through this. The oil field was growing. The fracking activity was starting to take off. We were in our own little bubble in the oil field and continued on with business as usual. Forte, who would have had to take on debt to acquire the business, stepped back from loans but stayed in communication. The discussions intensified around 2010.

The market at that point was heating up even further with the fracking activity, which at some point had to come to a peak. Supply forecasts were difficult to make. We did not try to guess the market. We used our own internal barometers to gauge progress.

Forte had actually contacted my partner Simon first and he had multiple phone conversations before I joined in. To him, Forte seemed like the right partner. They were very small for a publicly traded company, and we thought we could keep our uniqueness and wouldn't be swallowed up into a large steel company.

Something else was happening at this time. A number of customers were asking us to head to overseas locations. We looked into Dubai in the Middle East. This was leaving my entrepreneurial comfort zone as in Dubai, they will rent you the soil or sand and you have to make your investment into a building. You own the building, but you don't own the sand. The leases were very short term on the dirt, and the rules and regulations were so different from the United States on the structure and things. I wasn't comfortable with the amount of money it would take to invest overseas with a whole other set of laws.

There were customers saying, "If we're to grow with you, we really need an overseas location." We felt one thing Forte could offer was the infrastructure to leverage this opportunity. They already had overseas operations in England, France, Singapore, etc. We felt this would also be a way to move our footprint over there. With Forte's money, we would be more comfortable doing it.

So, that was the situation with the business. There were also personal or emotional sides of the deal.

My Personal Position

As I said, *everything is for sale at the right price.* Yet this is not to deny the emotional side to the process. Despite my philosophy, I went through this emotional stage. *This is getting real. Are we going to sell in these times?*

And yet I had several good reasons to want the sale, now it had been suggested. Personally, I felt I had plateaued. I'm not saying there wasn't anything new to learn in the steel business or in different ways to do things, but there was nothing obvious or immediate in sight. Business was good. We had a good sales staff. We could expand overseas, with or without a buyout. Everything was fine, but some of the day to day challenges weren't as great as they used to be. Even my relationship with Simon had hit a plateau and no longer offered opportunity for growth and positive change. In addition, around 85% of my net worth was tied up in steel inventory on the ground.

You can look at this situation in two ways. One is by getting a Schwab or Fidelity statement, meaning you hold a piece of paper. Sometimes, that doesn't seem very tangible. The other is when you can walk out on the ground and see your assets there. This *is* tangible, and nobody could take that away from you.

I think the BP Horizon explosion, which happened in 2010, also made me stop and think about my situation. We could have had a piece of steel in the BP Horizon and possibly been dragged into the lawsuit for failure of steel. Everything that I worked for over twenty years could have been taken away in a lawsuit if it was found to be a defect. I was getting older and had more networth lying on the ground. That also played a part in the decision-making process.

In addition to the plateau problem, I was diagnosed with colon cancer in September 2011. At this point, my partner Simon was leaning away from the point of selling. We both realized things would be different if we sold, and he wasn't sure how that would affect him in the future. For me, things were different already. The colon cancer meant I wanted to eliminate as much stress as I could from my life. Everything lined up at this point to make selling a tempting option. We had a peak in the market, and a need to expand overseas. I'd been in partnership with Simon for a quarter century. Having a partnership was stressful on both of us as we grew older and our priorities changed. I know I stressed Simon out and Simon stressed me out. Our association lasted longer than most, but at that point, it was probably time to step back and say, "Maybe a change would help alleviate this piece of stress, as well."

If we sold, we would have the ability to take our net worth and take it out of steel and put it into something else, offering new opportunities while leaving many current stresses behind. We could make a new beginning.

The Process of Selling

Once we'd made the decision to sell, I looked for some advice from my friend Steve Stephens, CEO of Amegy Bank. Steve and I have run together every Wednesday morning for fifteen years now. Our conversations have gone from business to personal and everything in between. I mentioned there was a possible contender thinking about purchasing our firm. Steve's advice at the end of the run that day was that I should talk to an Investment Banker.

This advice was reinforced by Steve Brody, my business mentor, to whom I talked inside my CEO group. He said it was not good to orchestrate our own sale because there would be emotions involved.

> **Talk to an Investment Banker**
>
> **There is a lot they can do for you during a transaction. They understand business sales. They've done them. They know all the things owners might overlook. Sure, they have fees, but more than likely you'll get back their fee in the sales price, so it's really a net benefit.**

I think Steve Brody made an excellent point when he mentioned emotional investment. Even when you're intellectually ready and willing to sell, there is bound to be an emotional tie to something you've worked so long to build up.

I heard stories from other business owners whose deals fell apart because these owners were negotiating their own deals. Sometimes they walked away from deals over stupid little things such as a $200 plaque on the wall. It wasn't the plaque on the wall that was the real problem. It was just one more thing, and the straw that broke the camel's back.

> **Investment Bankers**
> **Using an Investment Banker to negotiate the deal prevents all this and is absolutely great advice.**

Simon and I talked to a local Houston company called Growth Capital Partners (later acquired by Duff & Phelps.) We chose them because they had done many deals with

Amegy, and I trusted that relationship. Amegy, I knew, would not refer people to their clients if those people were not doing a good job. I got along well with David Sargent, who was one of the founding partners in that firm.

Because we found them to be such a good match, we did not look at other investment banking firms. The fact that they were local also influenced our decision. We could talk to everybody directly.

The Sale Process

Now it was time to make that sale. Both Simon and I had a certain number in mind, and this is where the investment bankers really helped out. Simon and I were pushing for another $4 million just because we liked the way the number rounded out in the sales price. The investment banker found out that the $4 million more probably would have stopped the whole process. The board had approved a maximum ceiling and the price we'd chosen was $4 million over that ceiling.

Simon and I thought, "We're up this far in numbers, what's another $4 million?" Well, it turned out another $4 million would have been a deal-breaker. So our banker saved us from spoiling our own deal, and things consequently went fairly well.

The process is not only between seller and buyer. There is also existing staff to consider. The buyer brought in a number of people and did a lot of management interviews and we did some offsite interviewing out of the office. That's when we realized this process would be hard on the employees. With strangers coming and going the staff knew something was up, they just weren't sure exactly what and how it would affect them.

Some employees asked directly if something was going on, and I answered it just as directly. I just didn't name companies and didn't let them know how deep we were in negotiation. Another company started looking at us during the same period. That meant more new faces coming in the office without introductions. When we had new contacts and new customers, of course, we generally introduced them to many people. When new faces came in and they didn't get introduced, it sent a message throughout the company. "Who are these people? Why are they coming through?"

Honesty

When a sale is in progress that will affect staff, I think honesty is the best policy. You don't have to tell them everything, but I think they deserve to know part of the process of what's going on. How much, what and when to tell them is unique to each company.

Process Timing

In terms of process timing, we got there very quickly. By March of 2011, everybody had agreed to everything, on both sides of the table. At that point, Forte ran into problems getting the money. They put everything on hold. I think Duff & Phelps thought they weren't going to get the deal done. When things stall like that, it affects the emotional component of the process. While a deal is stalled, you don't see the money in the bank yet. A deal is not a deal until it's done. We'd had light negotiations, then the financial crisis. Then, negotiations picked up again, we came to an agreement, and then, they couldn't find the money. We were in communication for about six months until late July when they got Davies, the financier, to start to commit to them on the negotiations. In August, we started documenting things and papering up drafts. Things were moving very quickly then from August to December. December 11 is when we closed everything.

Communicate with Your Law Firm

During a deal, make sure you have a great law firm that's close by. This is not a mom or pop transaction. Make sure your counsel has done these deals before and understands the structure, and can help you with your employment contracts. These things all have to be worked out. What management has to remain on contract and for how long?

We took care of every employee, and that took some planning. Some of those employees got a check with two commas in it.

The tax structure is not simple. The accounting firm has to work with the legal firm to make sure those checks are written in the best tax-effective way for both employer and employee.

In our case, negotiations with the buyers were very amicable. They wanted to be in the oil fields. They loved our business segment. We were 99% oil field and they wanted to add that to their pie. They were a $1.2 billion company and their size appealed to us. They were agreeable to the inventory and the way we presented it.

They didn't pick through anything and say, "Hey, this stuff is too old. You need to write it down."

It was a good match, I felt. The only problem area was when financial matters stalled and there was some doubt on whether they were going to be able to find the money and be able to do the deal.

The Day of Closing

On the day of closing have the cell phone number of everyone involved. Have all phone numbers to hand. This should include accountants, investment bankers, attorneys and everybody else involved in the deal. Office contacts are not enough. You need to be able to contact key people out of hours. An operator or an owner needs those numbers for anything that might go wrong in the last minute of the deal.

I thought the deal was done and went off to celebrate. I was on my second beer when I get a call and they said, "Hey, we can't fund without x document." I can't even remember what the document was. Our attorney had not seen the importance in it because the money was funded from Davies bank, but now came the news the bank could not fund until that document was filed. It had to be done that night. It took me a daisy chain of calling three different people to get our attorney's private phone number. At that point, he had to go into the office.

So the deal was done. I had a beer, and what were my feelings? There was this huge relief of just crossing the finish line. I hadn't looked at the bank account yet, so it wasn't "Wow! Look at that!" It was just about getting something completed. I thought we were there. After rushing around back in the office, scanning documents, and trying to put everything back together late at night, I finally got home after midnight. There was no emotion. I just wanted to lie down in bed. But then, the next morning I had to get up. The deal was done, but I got up as normal, heading into the office as normal. I checked the bank account, and saw the deposit was made. Then, it hit me like, "Wow." Wow can mean a lot of different things. Wow is like, "I don't own this anymore," "Wow, is that is a nice deposit."

Talking to Employees

Then came another challenge; talking to the employees.

Although I was as prepared as I thought I could be, I was way underprepared for the emotions on the employees' faces, and for the tears and the disbelief. They'd known something was in the air, but they didn't know the details. We called the entire company together to make the announcement. It went over like a lead balloon. There was nobody happy at all.

One of the books that Steve and I talked about is *Who Moved My Cheese?* We all voluntarily moved everybody's cheese and they were not happy about it. They knew their lives were going to change. We treated our employees very well. We provided good benefit packages, and lots of fringe benefits in the workplace, between lunches and Cokes and snacks. We always worked with employees to negotiate their time off, whether regular holidays or the sudden need to go and handle a sick kid. Those things might all change with the new owners, and everybody knew they would be different.

> **The piece of advice there is be as prepared as possible. Don't think any employees will embrace your euphoria over the closing. They're going to be feeling the complete opposite; upset, resentful and afraid of the future.**

That employee reaction was hard on me that day. In fact, it was so hard that I left early that afternoon. It was hard on the employees to go back to their desk as well.

Chapter Two: The Transition Begins

Transitioning from owner to employee of my former business was one area where Vistage had prepared me pretty well.

What is Vistage?

Vistage is an international organization of CEOs with about 20,000 members worldwide. It was founded on the principle of a Peer Advisory Group. It is lonely at the top, and the mission is to Increase the effectiveness and enhance the lives of CEOs. Membership appeals to people who believe in lifelong learning and growth and development. Meetings are probing, in-depth, challenging, and stimulating conversations to improve leadership habits and accountability. Groups are typically made up of 12 – 16 members. With about 1000 Groups in the US, each is run by a Vistage Chair, an experienced business advisor and CEO Coach.

I had watched how other firms in our Group have sold and have really struggled with working for their new ownership. I thought I had done enough homework with our new buyer, P.S. Forte, and had let them know I would help them in any way needed. I did not want to carry the title of President of the organization. Forte had a Houston office already with a President of the oil field division here in town. That made it easy on me in they already had a known President and he would be my boss. I was okay with that.

My role was not going to change significantly one way or another, except I didn't have the authority I had twenty-four hours ago. I was prepared for that mentally and I was okay with it. Unfortunately, my preparation couldn't insulate me against what happened within ninety days of the handover, when I got a role that I didn't want and was very clear that I didn't want.

The President of the oil field division had some management behavior that was reported to HR. HR flew down from the Denver corporate office to interview me and a bunch of other employees, and to hear directly what was going on from our point of view. As a result, they made the decision to let the President go. Thus I got a phone call at home on a weekend saying, "We need some help. Would you become President of this division?" This was the exact role that I didn't want. And yet, I felt obligated to help in any way I could.

One: I wanted to help my ex-employees, none of whom had left. I wanted to take care of them the best way we could. Two: Forte had paid a lot of money for our company, so I felt obligated.

The President's contract was terminated, and I stepped into the role now of the basic President of a public company, which in itself was a unique learning experience.

Exposure of Presidents

Presidents of public companies have to sign a lot of legal documents, and their salary becomes known to the world. Their picture goes on the website. You have to be prepared for this and for the recognition and exposure it brings.

It was so different for me. Now I was reporting to the CEO, and the board. But that wasn't all. Within 45 days the company decided to let the CEO go. The CFO became interim CEO. I went in a few weeks from 26 years of having just myself and Simon to report to into the situation of having three bosses. I had the President of the division, who was then let go. Then I had the CEO who was also let go. Then came a CFO. He and I got along well, and we are still in communication to this day.

Running through my mind was; "How did we miss all this? How could this happen?" How did this chain of events take place so fast? Was this going to happen anyway, even if we had not sold? Or did we take steps likely to bring this to a head? On reflection, this business experience wasn't really a negative for me, other than I got the job I didn't want. It was a great learning experience just to see how these transitions happened, and how new CEOs, and Presidents of divisions are here today gone tomorrow. One of the reasons I didn't want the position was that there's a skill set I do not have, and that's a clear understanding of financial statements. I struggle getting through them. Some people do have the ability to go through these and understand them easily.

As President of division, I had to make presentations to the board. Now I have this job and nobody to support me on this. I didn't have the public company knowledge I needed. It's one thing to sit down with a financial statement with a bank, and talk it over. I can handle that fine. This was different. This was to go through why there's x percent over one hundred and twenty days of receivable and what's your plan and all these boardroom discussions that result from it. Those are the things I didn't want, and now I had to try to figure out how to do them with no preparation. Also my computer skills are not great. Presidents of other divisions would plan on at least thirty days if not sixty days of putting together their PowerPoint presentations for the quarterly board meetings. And that just wasn't me.

I was thrown into it and I would say I got probably a C minus if not a D on handling that side of the job. I just did not do a very good job of it.

The Nature of Micro-Managing by Corporate

When we sold, we thought we'd done our homework. We didn't get anything in writing in some areas. For example, we thought we had everybody's agreement that Steel Inc would be left alone, and operate as its own division of Oil and Gas. We expected we would retain our own entity and our name and identity and just keep on going. That changed very rapidly. We were led to believe it would be two years before we started seeing any real change. Within thirty days the Forte letterhead appeared alongside ours. To me those were some small leaks in the dam. Then, our warehouse pay was probably 25% less than their warehouse pay. They wanted us to bring our guys up to their standards. I was thinking, "Man this is going to have a lot more cost every month and as long as the two groups operate separately, as we agreed, why do we need to do this?" This is just one example on where I fought about bringing our guys up to their standards. I lost that battle. They said there had to be one pay across the board.

There were other things. For example, we gave our guys a choice of uniforms. Because of the heat in Texas, they wanted to wear blue jeans with their uniform tops. They didn't want to wear the synthetic Dickies uniform bottoms that are extremely hot and not comfortable in the heat down here. Forte wanted standard uniforms throughout the company. Now, we've never had an eye accident, but we had implement eye wear, hard hats and all the things Forte used in our warehouse as well.

We were being told to do so many things. It seemed there was little freedom. I chose not to do some of those things, even though I was told to. Then when people would visit and say, "Where are the hard hats?" I'd say, "Over there in the box," or whatever. They'd go reporting back to the CEO and I would be scolded and told I had to get out the hard hats. The corporate safety guys just had to meddle in the way we did business. On the organization chart, I was definitely higher than them. Still, they would go back and talk to the CEO and then it would come back to me, and I would have to comply. I resisted many of these things along the way, but ultimately gave in.

Get it in Writing

When selling a business, don't ever assume you're on the same page or agreed on day-to-day matters. Always get the things you think both sides have agreed upon in writing. That way you have a reasonable bargaining point if they suddenly try to change the rules.

Regarding certain authority on purchases, that's the one thing that was left alone. When I finally left, it was starting to change, but for a good while they left this alone on most of our purchasing authority. We did have a few changes there though.

We were dealing with the small office supply firms that would bring product up the same day you ordered. Forte said, "No, you have to order it from Staples." We agreed. The problem was it would take a week to get in supplies now instead of getting them the same day. We could live with little things like that, by planning a bit more.

Then there was accounting. They started to chip away and say, "We're going to move accounting to Denver." Then they said, "You're going to have to change your software program. You're going to have to get on board with our software."

The software directive would be one that we fought the longest, and largely won. Because of the way we track our inventory and uniqueness, and our trace-ability, we never came anywhere close to half of 1% in error of inventory balances at year end. We did an inventory count and an audited statement. Our system was very accurate. We knew exactly what we had in the yard, and they did not. Their system did not track it well. So why would we want to change to something that was not accurate? That was our main point.

As things progressed, they would slowly take things like payables up to Denver. Now I still had authority. We would approve everything in Houston, and our expenditures were okay, but then payable started changing. Next, invoicing moved up there. Forte was slowly taking authority out of Houston, at a much faster pace.

Eventually, I left. We closed the deal in December of 2011, and I left in January of 2013. Shortly after that I think almost 100% of accounting was handled out of Denver.

> **Stay or Go?**
>
> **If a position in a company turns out to be markedly different from the one you agreed on before closing the deal, fighting back might work in the short term. Eventually, it might be better to draw a line and leave.**

Initially, I thought we'd done our homework, and I'd decided to be there for a long time. They were paying a great salary, and I was doing what I wanted to do. I expected to be more back into the sales and purchasing role, versus running the company.

Then, at the beginning of the third quarter of 2012, my fourth boss came along. Forte hired a gentleman who did freight for American Airlines. He had been one year out of work, and the headhunters found him, and he came in. In my opinion he had zero knowledge of distribution, and zero knowledge of the steel business. That doesn't mean he's not a smart man, but I detected a little bit of arrogant behavior. He was very clear on who was the boss in the room, and very clear with me on, "You will comply, you will do things that we tell you to do, and you need to start getting them done now."

To me, that fourth boss was the beginning of the end. I could not relate to him. After sitting one entire quarter with him, I'd had enough. It was a little before Thanksgiving, and I said, "Frank, what I signed up for was to work in the oil field division, not to be President of it. You're my fourth boss, and that was not in anything I signed up for." I said, "Frank, I'll give you an entire year's notice or I'll give you one day if that's what you want. I need to leave. I'm not in a hurry to leave, and I don't want to leave on bad terms. Just let's sort out the notice and I'm outta here, I'm gone. You decide on how long you want me around."

After he slept on it for a weekend, he said, "Would you stay until the end of next quarter?"

That's how I ended up staying through the end of January 2013. Part of the problem was that the rules of the game had changed. It was different from what I had planned on and from what I believed we had agreed.

There was another problem, too. After two years, Forte renewed my contract and they told me they were not going to renew Simon's contract. I said, "Frank, that's fine, that's your decision. You need to tell Simon." And he said, "No, he reports to you on the organization chart, so you need to tell him."

This was a very interesting situation. I had to sit down with a man who was my equal 50/50 partner for 26 years, and all of a sudden I had to tell him he needed to go. That was very hard on me emotionally. Even though we've had disagreements, to walk in a room and tell my long-time partner that I had to let him go was not a good place to be for either of us. Simon knew it wasn't my decision, and he took it very well.

Forte wanted me in a management meeting in Denver on my last day. This was one more thing that was handled poorly. They weren't finished in the meeting, and I had to catch my flight back to Houston. I stood up and just started closing my books. I waved goodbye to everybody and the CEO said, "Goodbye." The IT guy said, "Is he leaving?" And someone said, "Yes."

That's literally how Frank let me go. I just walked out the door; it was just another day, just another employee for him. Knowing I was going to leave for a quarter, I was very sensitive not to send off any bad signals around the room, so I didn't make any moves until I was about to leave. I didn't even take family pictures off my desk.

Now, I'm a pack rat. After 26 years of collecting papers on my desk and in my drawers and information about producing steel metals and things, I literally had hours the next day to pack up all those years, and to get in the car and leave. Forte wanted me out of the facility right now. So, I came back from Denver.

The next day I was at the office at my regular time, and I made the announcement.

It was less of a shock to people to learn that I was leaving than when they learned I'd sold. Still, it was extremely emotional that day as well.

In thinking about handling the conversation with my people, I think it's one of those moments in my life where I have a memory lapse. It was such a strong emotional day to walk in knowing I owned the building still. I walked out of a building that I owned, but I didn't own anything on the inside anymore. I took my parking spot sign and put in my car. The employees got that for Simon and me about our 20th anniversary. Our parking lot was so congested and that was a very thoughtful gift. That sign meant a lot to me, because it came from the employees. I had pulled pictures off the walls, and awards I received from companies, and customers, and from vendors. I put those all in boxes and took them home. It was a tough day, and that's why I think I was just numb.

I don't think there were many tears when I was leaving. How should I take that? People were happy to see me go or what? Of course the corporate announcement came out. I don't remember if they made the announcement before I did.

Be Prepared

Be prepared. Outline exactly what is going to happen after closing. Don't depend on a verbal undertaking to leave the business alone for two years, or to retain contacts or staff. Instead, make these agreements and put them in writing, signed by both parties. If the guidelines say, "We'll be in your business taking it over, accounting and everything in 90 days," so be it. That means both sides fully agree on that timeline. Something else to be clearly established in writing is how authority levels will work post-closing.

When I went into it initially, authority levels really didn't seem to apply to me. Therefore I thought they didn't matter to me. I wasn't going to own the business. I wasn't going to be President.

Signing Authority

If owners are going to be kept on as President, I think their authority level needs to be very clear cut, in writing. Not just, "Oh, yeah, yeah. Things will be the same as they always have been," because they're not. I've seen some of my fellow Vistage members start off with $25,000 signing authority for guys that used to sign for half a million/one million dollar contracts easily. Signing authority needs to be worked out, and it has to be specified when it needs to be dual authority. Where are those levels? What is the approval process?

I found Houston's Forte locker room to be atrocious. I would not give my dog a bath in that place. It was horrible. It was black, it was moldy, it was humid and it was just nasty. This was the work environment for those employees. So—I did what I've always done to improve conditions. I hired a contractor, and they said, "Did you get approval for that?" "No I didn't get approval on that. "Well, anything over $50,000 needs three signatures I was told."

I found out I could sign up to $25 000, so I had the contractor break the contract into two pieces. That way I could sign for both pieces of the contract and get it done and keep it moving.

Before you Sign

Before you sign, get it clearly understood, in writing, how much responsibility you can take for signing and decisions. Remember, things that you normally would do as soon as you made the decision now might need to be officially approved.

Had I gone the formal route and gone all the way through how it needed to be done, it would have been 90 to 120 days before we could've started construction to get all the proper approvals and some metals into the corporate office to get that locker room renovation done. So again, it just comes back to simple rules of engagement, and that was one example.

Here's an example: you might have a relationship with Joe's Sandwich shop that brings sandwiches over every Friday for everybody. This might end or change with new owners. In healthcare and retirement programs, ours were similar to Forte's, but there were major changes for the employees once we switched over. Adjustments had to be made. There was total confusion both on the HR side and on the employee side on people that were starting to meet their insurance deductible or had met the deductible requirements. Now they were on a new plan and this became confusing. How do you resolve the employee considerations? These sound like simple things, but they really start to add up as you get in, working together.

What about Medical?

More homework is needed upfront on how you're going to handle the change in medical. If you're changing plans, how are you going to handle the employees with their deductibles to date? Once again this needs to be in writing, so there's a working document of how after closing, these things will be handled. A lot of time needs to be spent on that.

Employment Contracts

In our deal, management being on board with employment contracts was very important to Forte. They wanted everybody's employment contract signed prior to closing. That was part of the deal. It was one of those things that caught me off guard, one of the things that I thought would be minor, but which turned out to be very major.

Almost each management contract had to be individually negotiated. Even though our managers knew they would be well taken care of with a financial reward, having them sign a two year employment contract was one of the most difficult things of the entire transaction. It came down to two managers that were really holding out. At one point, I was thinking, "How ironic is this? We've agreed to a price, the owners have agreed to their work contracts, and literally we might lose this deal because of two managers."

I don't know if Forte truly would've walked away from the deal had those guys not signed but that's the card they were playing during negotiations.

Get Your Managers on Board

Don't take lightly getting your managers on board if they're going to be required to sign a work contract. Be prepared to negotiate each one individually. Do it as early in the process as you can.

That's what happened to us. Each guy had some uniqueness for his needs. Some said, "Fine, looks good to me. I'm staying here no matter what. Thanks," signed it and moved on. Then came these two hold outs. It looked as if we would lose the deal because of two hold outs. You need to be prepared for that.

In most acquisitions, there is provision to have management stay on board. That needs to be done early on. Here we were, literally days before closing, still working things out. So don't let that be part of the hang up of closing.

Chapter Three:
Loyalty to Prior Team Members

Post sale, just to jump ahead, we wrote a check to everybody. From floor sweepers, cleaning people, and all, we gave everybody a "thank you for being with us" gift. Some of those checks were a few hundred dollars, and some as I stated had two commas in them. The people who got two commas in them were, in Simon's and my opinion, part of the driving force of Steel Inc. Even though Simon and I had a skill set, without these guys' skill set brought into the mix we would have never got to where we were.

> **Thank your people**

In terms of large payouts, there were, I guess two. Then there were a few more with significant amounts awarded. Phantom stock was used as the basis for these awards. This was a certain % of the value of the transaction, that was rewarded. The two larger rewards were in writing, and below that, everybody else was just discretionary. We felt that even for the cleaning lady, we had to morally include a thank you for maintaining things throughout; for good housekeeping around the place. So we took good care of everybody.

One of the hardest things to do was saying goodbye to those people in the sense that I was no longer their boss. Then it comes back to their cheese getting moved, and I'm the one that moved it. Part of me for the longest time was having a hard time dealing with that.

Guilt over Moving the Cheese

Someone said, "Did you pay those people a fair wage over the entire time they worked for you?" I said, "Yeah." He said, "Would you have paid them more than a fair wage?" I said, "Well yeah, a lot of people." And we got into some of the bonuses and things. Then he said, "Did you ever directly promise that they would always have employment with you?"

He went through this series of questions with me, and essentially it came down to this: "So do you think that if somebody came along and offered them double their income, they would have any loyalty to you? Would they as an employee say, 'Oh no, Patrick's taking good care of me, I'll pass on 50% or double my pay.'" And I said, "Probably not." And he said, "So you've had a payday, and you've taken good care of them along the way. Where does the loyalty start and stop? You took care of yourself. You didn't make promises that you didn't live up to. You need to say, 'I kept my commitment to them, and I never made them a promise that it was for employment forever.' Then you remember you had people leave over the course of time when it suited them."

So I got it, and as simple as that sounds, it was hard to get because of one thing we tried to differentiate ourselves. Both Simon and I had worked for a big company, and we saw how they treated employees of the company. We were determined to be different and we were different. We were more of a business family, and to break up that family is what was happening.

> **Loyalty to Employees**
>
> **Remember: you promised your employees a fair wage for a fair day's work. You never promised them employment forever.**
>
> **Remember: If a better offer came along, they would probably take it, so why shouldn't you?**

There were retention contracts or bonus payments to various people. They stayed on. One of them completed his work contract and just left. He also did not like the new management structure. Charles was our CFO, and left without a job, because he had enough of the changes. I think it was more frustrating for Charles than for anybody else to deal with. Mainly it was the reporting structure and the numerous details. Charles was very professional about the changes. For the transition period, he was willing to help out because a lot of accounting activities were completed from this office.

 We spent a lot of time training the replacement for Charles. Then after I left, it was harder on others. Simon and I were both gone. Once the non-compete contracts ran out, then Charles took a position with another firm similar to Steel Inc.

His work contract included a one year non-compete. He had one year before he could do a similar job. In the meantime, he just did some financial consulting for some small companies. I guess he was mentally preparing to go into competition.

After I left it seemed to trigger a number of folks to leave. At Charles's new company, there are four of the seven of our management staff now working.

Now they're all gone from our company. There's nobody from the existing management staff left. The Forte style was just a problem. I'd say anybody that felt employable left with or without jobs secured. Some who left already had a position. Others just said, "I can't take it," and then left. The people that stayed over there were either older or just didn't get a job somewhere else. I don't know the full reason. Maybe they just didn't want to change.

The Business Unit

The Business Unit changed. They closed down the Forte office and moved everybody over to the Steel Inc facility. We operated out of two plants while I was still there. Accounting comprised two different software and accounting packages. After I left, they brought everybody together and merged as just one.

What was the effect on the business after we left? Well, even on the public calls on quarterly financially calls of Forte, to my knowledge they still track this internally on what the Steel Inc division does. For a couple of quarters they kept separate records. Now this is pure speculation, but I think sales fell to half of what they were. I know the employee numbers were halved. We had over 100 employees, and they're down to 41. The staff has been reduced dramatically.

How do all these changes or reductions make me feel? At this point I've passed the emotional side of it. It's hard for me to believe that they paid prime dollar to buy an asset that was doing well, and then they chose to immediately change that. So there; I can't help but still to this day feel a little emotional about what took Simon and me 26 years to build up. The new owner has knocked it down in just a couple of years to a fraction of the size. It is sad that it took 26 years to build it up and two or three years to tear it down. Very sad.

Would I like to see my legacy continue? Yeah, I guess I would. "Hey, I thought of that thing over there." Nowadays that's probably not going to happen. It's not what it was. I'm over the emotional piece of that now. At this point it's just sad, that somebody paid a lot of money for a business, and they don't have the benefit of what they paid for.

Walking Away

If you've done a fair deal, you have to walk away from your prior firm. What happens to it after you leave is up to the new owners.

Chapter Four: Personal Assets, Trusts, Financial Planning, and Protection

Let's think of the many financial considerations that needed to be made. We'll cast our thoughts back to the day after settlement, going into work the next day, logging into the bank account, and seeing a very large deposit has been made. What do you do next?

The first thing you think about is, "Wow how is that protected?"

Go with a large bank. It could have problems, but it's less likely.

Protecting Your Deposit

FDIC insurance goes up to $250,000. Essentially anything above $250,000 sits there unprotected. Just addressing that I think you want to be with a sizable bank. When choosing an investment broker, don't choose someone new. Use someone with whom you have a good track record.

For us the sale was a public record because we sold to a public firm. Brokers from coast to coast started calling. The broker calls were just unbelievable. It was just, "Hey I see you had a transaction. We're so and so, we've handled high networth individuals," and on it went.

I didn't take notice of these cold calls. Instead, we went back to the people who handled our retirement account, which happened to be Lawrence and Partners. For ninety days minimum, or it might have even been six months, we did nothing. We just took that money and we split it up within Amegy Bank, some in mutual funds and other investments.

After that time passed, we moved some monies over to Lawrence and Partners. A portion went to them, another piece to mutual funds, etc.

We got to know the banks' trust department. Within the trust department there's an investment group that can handle this kind of money. We went in to meet the people, got introduced, and understood the team. We sat down and they asked what our comfort levels were with various risk profiles. We designed a plan for the family. We decided nothing changes. Lawrence and Partners has the same investments that we had, just with larger dollars.

I've left a third drawing a quarter of 1% interest, yielding hardly anything. This third of those monies still sits out there just as a liquid asset. It's a security blanket for me, and it's readily accessed if something would come along. There have been people that have rushed into the market and the market changed and they lost a lot of capital.

A good example is Charlie E. (a business associate.) Duff & Phelps talked him out of rushing to make investments after his company sale. So he didn't get into the market as soon as he wanted. In that interim, the market took a huge drop. Not getting the money moved as fast, actually saved him quite a bit.

We went to a good attorney, sat down and laid out what our family's net worth was, and how we were going to move some things around. We updated wills very promptly after the sale. I guess you could do it before the sale if you actually know what's going to happen. We did ours promptly afterwards. This was in conjunction with our accounting service so we had joint meetings where Marks Partners and the advisors came together. We brought in the life insurance company and had a three way meeting to review options. Everybody was together working as a team to make sure this was laid out properly. One of the things the IRS allows you to do is to give some money to your children. The number moves a little bit every year, but it's roughly five million dollars per child. Structured properly, it passes without estate tax.

The Building

Forte did not want the buildings, so Simon and I still owned one building in Canada and two in Houston. We had an official valuation of those properties done, and got a certified report. With that, then we became the general partners owning a half percent each. The other 99% of the warehouses belongs to our sons. The valuation of that worked out to roughly 20 million dollars. There were four sons, my two and Simon's two, and that amount transferred to the boys. That took a huge a piece of net worth out of my and Simon's portfolio. It allows it to move on down to the next generation tax free. We wrote a trust based on our side. There's a trustee and at the age of thirty, our boys become co-trustees. They start to get more involved, and the monies that come from that can be used for health, for education, for housing and living standards. It doesn't fall into the area of buying aircraft, summer homes or things of that nature.

The cash that comes from rentals are reinvested into the boys accounts. They are now owners of parts of some apartment complexes. This will continue to grow within those long-term investments.

We've involved the boys in those conversations, and they understand that their trust owns parts of these buildings. I would highly recommend that. Again it takes a huge chunk of your networth and you can move it to them to avoid paying tax. Simon and I had buy/sell agreements on shares, previously established. This type of financial planning was valuable advice from our experts.

> **Insurance**
>
> **Don't let your insurance policies lapse. I think you need to be aware of the value in those and have them worded to protect assets and the other partners left behind.**

We purchased these insurance policies at a younger age. In my case, having cancer affected my ability to increase any of these. With these policies you might feel you have enough money, and your family has enough money but you can not be sure.

You can put those into a trust, or you can donate them to a church or temple, or organizations. You continue to pay the premiums, but upon your death, then somebody is rewarded with the money. I would say make use of them, review those policies and see if some good can come from it for someone else.

Family Life after the Sale

Ann and I discussed things with the boys, as I said. Four years ago, when we set up the trusts, they were twenty-one and seventeen. The sale information is public record so they could have figured it out on their own, had we chosen not to say much about the value. But we're a fairly open household anyway, so we shared with them the event and the amount. We were just as open through the whole process as we could be. In fact Jack, after graduating went to work as an intern just for a couple of weeks at Duff & Phelps doing some spreadsheets and things. It was a nonpaid, position in their office.   He now understood what an investment banker did.

The boys, who are both pretty deep thinkers, mostly listened and took in facts from these discussions. They have not asked many questions along the way. We've been involved with attorneys' meetings to understand how the wills work. We made sure they know where our passwords are and things of this nature. If there was an event where both Ann and I are gone, I didn't want it to turn into a crisis for them.

While our boys were getting ready to begin employment, I didn't want them to think they had any obligation to come into the family business. I wanted them to know they had to go off and find their own desires. That was another reason to sell. They didn't have to worry about coming into the family business because it isn't there anymore.

Neither did they want to go on any spending sprees. They have worked through college in the summer. So they're not out being playboys and doing nothing; they're making good use of their time. I think that comes from inside the home. It would be selfish on our part to say, "You don't need to work. Come on home, you don't need to do that, there's plenty of money here, just come on home and enjoy the summer and relax." Ann and I ask them to go find a job in the summer time.

We have not made any significant lifestyle changes, so I suppose the boys followed that example. We have made some additions and land acquisitions here at the farm. I did splurge on a big, green tractor. I bought a $125,000 Jack Deer. When I saw the closing coming I put it on order, and it got delivered the month after closing. That is the one thing I did for myself.

Aside from that, we've had zero lifestyle change except that we always fly first class now. A guy I know said, "Fly first class, because if you don't your kids will." I thought that was a great line. Ann and I don't really want for much.

Ann

How did Ann look at things? My wife is even keeled. When I was considering business number two, the brewery, she was so supportive the entire way. Even though she admitted afterwards that it had gotten out of hand as far as the size I was planning. When I said "I'm not going to build it," all she said is, "Thank God." I love her to death, and appreciate how she'll give feedback when you ask. If you don't ask, she's not in your face about it. Through the selling process, she understood the reasons why we sold and supported those.

She understood it had to do with the cancer, the timing of the market, and all the reasons we talked about. How does Ann feel about me being round the house? A lot of spouses would have said, "Oh my God. I'd wish you'd go get another job." Ann, doesn't even seem to know I'm home. I try to let her live her lifestyle as she pleases. I think once you're home you can really interfere with your spouse's routines. My wife has a set of routines, so do I.

I get up at 5:30, work out, have some breakfast, read the paper, come back and go to my office and work. I just quietly sit in the office. If she needs help with something I'm there, but otherwise I'm away from her daily routine.

> **Living and working at Home**
>
> **Once the sale is completed, you might be spending more time at home. If so, it's important to have a routine. Your spouse or partner probably has one already, and it is much better if you don't get in the way.**

You'll hear more about Ann's perspective, straight from her, in Chapter Seven.

Requests for Donations

The sale information was public, so did we get lots of calls from people asking for donations? Not really. The news didn't seem to get out to the charitable area. We live a pretty low key lifestyle. I don't know if that has anything to do with it, but we seem to stay under the radar.

Regarding friends and family all of sudden besieging us... It has really not happened. One thing that happened was one of my sister's friends had too many cocktails one night. "I understand you're rich," she said. And I said, "You're right. I'm rich with love, I'm rich with family, I'm rich with life." How do you even respond to something like that?

Preparing for Tomorrow

I don't think you can move fast enough on getting things in place. You don't know what tomorrow will bring and whether you'll be alive or not. Once you've had a liquidity event, and then just moved pieces all over the place, somebody else is going to have to pick that up.

I have a journal book with tabs on it. In it I have real estate investments and security investments written by hand. I have a note that this is our account number at Lawrence and Partners. We have a safety deposit box at the bank. Then I have the approximate dollar amount. One simple example is how would my kids know that we bought CDs out of the Regional Texas Bank? It might come up sooner or later. But in this simple Office Depot journal, a bound journal, just with lines on the page, we've put in tabs to point the way. We've written in there where monies are parked, and how to access things. The boys know where to find it. It's crude, but it would help organize somebody if something happened to me or Ann or both of us.

Bank Trust Department

One of the resources we did not know existed was the bank trust department. We discovered they will review all documents free of charge. This helps to understand what the attornies had prepared.

From a mechanical standpoint this person just says, "I think these are in order." Or, "This might need another review."

There's a resource there where another set of eyes handles this every day. They can make suggestions to help you get a little more organized. I would say, reach out for those.

Tangible Assets

While we had the business, having inventory meant security. To go from that to a piece of paper was hard. One of the tangible things Ann and I have done is to invest in multi-family apartments. We've invested heavily in different projects around the city. One, it's an asset that you can drive by and see, and the returns from those are pretty good; somewhere between 8 and 12% depending on the unit. They are good long term investments. They are not liquid, so you've got to be prepared, but it was one other area besides the stock market in which we've parked a fair amount of money.

You need to feel comfortable with the groups, and we did research on a number of groups. From these, we chose three groups where we invested. We were able to meet the founders and some of the clients, their relationships, etc.

Tangible Assets

If you prefer tangible assets to virtual funds, consider buying into a variety of building projects such as multi-family apartments. Research the ownership groups to choose a comfortable match.

Chapter Five: Startup of a New Idea or Company (called Newco)

I won't take credit for the idea for Newco. Instead, I have to give credit to Ann. I consumed a lot of beer in my lifetime, and had always enjoyed going to breweries. I'd never wanted to home brew, and never wanted to be part of a brewery. I just enjoyed watching it being made in breweries around the world.

Ann's Suggestion

We were on a family reunion in Oregon when we stopped at a brewery called "Full Sail." Go into "Full Sail," someone said, so we did, and we had one of the best tour guides. This is a guy that's pulling out the different grains and, saying, "Smell this," And he just says, "Taste this." If you taste the flavor that's far better than if he just walked us through the brewing equipment. After we finished with the tour, we went in the bar and had a couple of glasses of ice cold beer. The salmon were running, so we had a great meal there also in the restaurant. And Ann looked at me, and she said, "Maybe this ought to be your next life?" And I said, "Put me in charge of the brewery?" "Oh my God, no way," "I'd drink all the profits." Anyway, that's where the seed started, on that tour. The tour was good, it was fun, and it was a beautiful day. That was all. The seed was planted.

We came back to Houston and I was doing the organizational things, just getting my life in order. I woke up every morning without an office to go to. There were things to do, but it's not as if I had to be at the office to get my job done. So it was that this idea that Ann planted grew. I had time on my hands, and my mind started to think of building again. I think we feel like we need to be busy. We've got time, and I thought, "Heck, I could build a brewery. Wouldn't it be fun to have a brewery out in the country?" So a piece of land came available, and I said, "Hey Ann, there's that farm land just outside of the city limits there. What do you think about a location for a brewery there?" She said, "Okay." So we bought 58 acres. It was farmland, so we were making hay on it. We had some cattle on it, so we were making use of it in the meantime.

The location was set, and so I started thinking about the brewery more, and this was an area I knew nothing about. I started to talk to people, went on a few more tours and met a group. "You need to join the Brewers Association," they said. "You need to join this and this." I started to know and talk to more people and found out there was a convention coming up in April. I went to the convention, and walked around.

Conventions

At this point, we secured the land, and had an idea of the size of the brewery. I talked to enough people. I just told Ann, "I am going to go to this convention, and I'm going to buy the Porsche, the Cadillac, the Mercedes—whatever you want to use as an analogy—of brewing equipment." I started walking the aisles. That's one of the things I always did at the oilfield show, the OTC in Houston; I was methodical about walking every aisle. You never know what's on some aisle that you might miss. So I did the same thing; I laid out a route, and walked every aisle. I had a list of people at the show I wanted to stop and see. By the second day, I realized I had no business buying anything. The more time I spent in those aisles, the more I realized I didn't know what I was doing. Even though I'm a business guy, and was used to doing deals, that did not mean I understood the brewery business. I finished the aisles on the third day and came home, not dejected, but just confused. I didn't know where to turn to get the information. One of the German manufacturers of brewing equipment that I stopped by to see did a follow-up sales call two months later. I said, "I like your equipment, but I don't know that yours is any different from anyone else's." They said, "We've worked with a company called First Key." They gave me the contact information, and I talked to them.

First Key

First Key is a consulting group of ex big beer executives and marketing guys and brew masters. I met with them, and they said, "We can create a plan from as little help as you need, to as much help as you need. We can walk you through a marketing study, which will start as a brewery and pretty much will expand as you want."

This is great, I thought; this is what I'm looking for. I signed up for the full program with them, and started off in an area I knew nothing about: marketing.

At Steel Inc, we never advertised; it was all word of mouth. We'd make sales calls, but we never did ad campaigns or anything like this. I started touring around with one of the First Key marketing guys. We would visit breweries and distributors all over the state, and try to understand where the craft beer market's going, and this worked into a business plan. First Key came back and said, "Our recommendation is to be this size brewery. This is the capital you're going to need. This is the cash it's going to throw off." I looked at this and I said, "Wow, this is really neat." So then the entrepreneur in me kicked in. To me, the bottom line has been a benefit but I've been more involved in the chase than the kill. Even though the consultant was telling me the money that can be made, I was more involved with building the brand and getting it into the market place. The initial funding was a whole new area. That for me was the new chase. I wanted to know how to create the label, how to create the flavors and profile of the beer, and then how to get it into the marketplace. Then, there was the equipment, and that's another side I wanted to touch on.

The Learning Curve

I really enjoy building things.

These things included our steel warehouses, and our home. I built three steel warehouses, and our home. I liked the input you're able to get with architects; the dream you start with and then just see it come from your mind to be an erected structure. It's a bit funny actually. You create a manufacturing plant, then you're making product, and it comes in with water and grain. Now you come out with a beverage at the other end. How you get to that product was just fascinating.

The learning curve was going straight up, and I enjoyed every day of learning this. That was really, really fun. Along the way on one of our tours, we met a young man from Houston who trained in Germany to become a brew master. As conversation went along, I said, "Kaleb would you like to come and work for a brand new company?" And, he said, "Yeah, it intrigues me." So Kaleb and I were getting more into the conversation, and one day Kaleb called me up and said, "I quit my job." "Kaleb, that probably wasn't the smartest thing to do" "You're lucky I'm a fair man," I said. "When you get back from your vacation," "we'll sit down and arrive at a salary. But you're a little ahead of the curve here.

So not by my choice, I got an employee, earlier than I anticipated. Now in hindsight, it actually worked out pretty well, because he started attending meetings and would give input on beer profiles. He'd come to the architectural meetings, and say, "No you can't do this, you should have this over here." In conjunction with the consultants, he turned out to be an asset.

Next I got an office in a secretarial suite. So now I had an office, an employee, and bank accounts starting to set up. Newco was starting to come to life. It was becoming a real company.

I hadn't quite fully finished with my organization after the sale, and I was now working at least a full forty hours a week on the brewery. I put some of the final little things that needed to get done for us personally, after the liquidity event, and just put those on hold. Newco had to get going; I had to get this done. That was just the entrepreneur in me. I just couldn't wait to get up every morning to get to the next thing we were working on. I really enjoyed that. With the entrepreneur it seems, the seed continues to grow. The more market study we did, the more it seemed you could sell almost any volume you could create. We were seeing this from coast to coast.

The brewery concept got up to probably five times the initial concept in size and volume. The building went from a small 10,000 square foot plant to 80 or 90,000 square feet. Another aspect of the brewery had a dance hall. Another learning was, why do Czechs and Germans build these? How do they build them? There's a whole history here. And then, how do you emulate this with modern structure, with air conditioning and things? None of these old ones were air conditioned. And how do you create the feel of an old dance hall? And what does the bar look like? What does the dance floor look like? What is the view? And all these were different. We worked a lot on that. And then we thought of a restaurant. So we had a brewery, we had a restaurant, and we had a dance hall. This idea that started off as just a brewery now had three businesses on the same property. It had both the nightclub or dance hall and a restaurant. We saw the need, because of the remote location, to make sure people had some food with their alcohol. Plus the area out here needed it. It just needed a restaurant, and then there was the brewery. So in my mind, those were three totally different businesses.

They all worked together, but, then came the first shock for the entrepreneur. I saw the estimated building cost, and that number was up so high that it had gotten out of hand. I would say that I was 99% of the problem. The other people on the team did a check and said, "Hey, I know you said you wanted a building that's big, but do you know that we've now exceeded your project by a little bit? We were 30-35% over what I had planned to spend. And I put everybody on hold.

That point was the first check, and I wanted to hit pause. This project had gone into tens of millions of dollars. I believed in the investment, so instead of getting a portfolio statement, I just thought, this is a true asset that's going to do a lot of things. One, I thought it'd be great for the community out here. And I love that aspect of being able to give back to the community. And two, it was going to give a return on an investment.

Then, in a meeting one day, the project manager let me know we went through the top end of my mental budget. I said, "This is my threshold. I'll spend up to this point."

At work, I pulled him aside, and I said, "Bob, what do you mean we've gone through that budget?" And he said, "Over what we thought." And I said, "What is the cost?" And he said, "I don't know, let me do some math, and I'll get back to you." He got back to me, and we were 35% above my threshold. And I said, "Wow."

I have to take at least 99% of the blame for this. Somebody's got to take 1% along the way here. I'll take 99%, just because I'm the entrepreneur. If I can sell one barrel I can sell ten barrels, and it's great. I went home and slept on that, and I called him up the next day. I said, "Bob, I want to put a hold on this." And he said, "Why?" And I said, "this has just gotten much larger than I anticipated, and I want to step back for somewhere between 30 to 90 days." He said, "Well that's very difficult to do." And I said, "Why is that very difficult to do, Bob?" And he said, "Well everybody on the architectural team is ready. I have First Key and all these people; the train's in motion. We've turned down other work because we're busy with this work. So if you say to hold for 90 days what is this team supposed to do? We have businesses to run. And again, we've turned down other work. We can't do nothing."

"Okay. I understand what you said. Let me sleep on this again, Bob."

So I'm a pretty dedicated guy. As I needed a brewer, I took a brewer on. And I took on other employees when I probably shouldn't have through the years. I understand the team needing to have income. So I just sat down with them and said, "We have to find a way to break down and lower the cost."

I allowed everybody to keep working. Yet, on breaking that threshold, all of a sudden something had changed in my mind. It just broke the "This doesn't feel right," threshold. After all, this is a second career and I want it to be fun, but the hours had gone way beyond 40 hours per week. I guess I was creeping into somewhere between 60 and 70 hours a week working. I mean it was all-consuming. We had friends and family call, and say, " Let's go to dinner," or, "Let's go here for the weekend." And I couldn't, because I had this new business. I had to work.

Ann understood, and was okay, because I could do work anywhere. We could come to the farm, and I could do the work. I could get up early in the morning. Her observation on this is at Steel Inc, my sleep pattern would be typically this: I would go to bed somewhere between nine and ten, and get up between midnight and two in the morning. Work for a couple of hours, then go back to sleep for a couple of hours. That sleeping pattern had changed since I sold the company. Now that sleeping pattern returned. I was getting up in the middle of the night, working, because the mind's going. And then I'd go back to bed. So those patterns were starting to come back again. And she just made note of it. She said, "You know you're getting up and working? I can hear you during the night." Quite frankly, it had just happened, and I didn't even think anything of it, because I'd done it for so many years. So the work patterns of yesteryear, of Steel Inc era, were returning and again, they crept up over sixteen months or so and evolved into this. I enjoyed being busy, and I was very busy and I was learning. But until Ann made note of that, I hadn't really realized I returned to my old habits. And once she said that, it started a second set of wheels turning.

Number one, the budget was too high. Number two, the hours were growing. This led to the thought, "Is this a hobby or is it a business?"

Is this a Hobby or a Business?

When you think about beginning a new project, especially one with a big outlay in time and money, ask yourself if it's a hobby or a business. A hobby might make money, or it might not, but if you intend to make money and if you can't walk away from it for weeks at a time then it's a business.

Now, the farm is more of a hobby for me. It is an operating company, a working farm, with employees that show up every day, but it's also a hobby. I can come and go, and the wheels keep turning whether I'm here or not. I can come and play cowboy or farmer, or whatever I want to do for the day. Then I can go back to Houston and spend time as I wish. So I view the farm as a working hobby.

Now coming inside the city limits of Houston, and looking at building a brewery, that is different. There are the regulations around alcohol, the investment, and the amount of capital. Things have to happen sequentially, and on a regular basis. You can't just come out, brew beer one month and then not distribute it and not ship it for a month. And then decide I'm going to make some more beer." So the brewery was beyond a hobby. It had legs to it and it had to repeat on a regular basis. If you wanted to call it home brew, then that could be done as a hobby. If you want to share it with friends, that's a hobby. This was a true business no matter what the size, whether it was going to be the one barrel company or the ten barrel company. It was beyond a hobby, from day one.

I'm not saying some businesses could be treated as hobbies or you'd actually be able to run it like the farm. If you wanted a hamburger stand and had a manager who's going to run it, sure you could say, "I own a hamburger stand and it's a hobby." But this brewery to me had things that needed to be attended to every day, almost seven days a week. Most breweries run seven days a week around the clock. It's a 365 day a year job. It was a real business, no matter what the size.

I was about to hit a wall with the business preparation. With the beer consulting company, along with the business projects also came an employee projection; bodies. It was going to be three business units. I'd planned to have all three up and running day one. So then I start adding up people to run the dance hall, people to run the restaurant, people to run the brewery. That head count, the way I added it up came to somewhere between 30 and 40 people on day one. So then I start to think about Steel Inc, on how it took fifteen years or so to get to 40 people. So first it's secretaries, and then warehousemen. And over the years, we would add bodies, and some years we had more than others. But it wasn't on day one.

All this had been fun, learning about the beer business, the equipment, advertising, and architects. Planning all this was fun, but then came the reality of having to hire 40 people. When we set a date to break ground, and another date to be open, reality set in. A part of that was going through the budget. That was a mental setback. And then I added up how many people I'm going to need. And that started to move me into another phase of, "Wow, I think I'm busy now but soon I'm *really* going to be busy." Then my mind went to, "Okay, I'm working in the office, it's five o'clock, I want to head home. I'd come downstairs, and let's just say the restaurant's packed and understaffed that night. Or for whatever reason, the bar is backed up and they can't pour beer fast enough. Do you really think Patrick is going to turn his back and continue walking out that front door? No he's not. He's going to put down his briefcase, get behind the bar, starting a conversation, start helping out, start doing whatever he does. And so then we're going back to "it's not a hobby." It's a full time job. And serving alcohol has other complications: legal, liabilities, many regulations. This was sounding quite complicated.

Why didn't I think about that in the very beginning? I'm a slow learner on some of these things. I get so wrapped up in building the business and learning all the different aspects. Employees were needed, I thought we could hire them later. So now, it seems we are over budget.

Pause at Belize

We had purchased a trip to Belize at a charity auction. We had scheduled it long before coming to this point. And so here we were, about ready to take off, and I didn't take any paper work with me. I brought my computer, and a couple of books, and I was just going to Belize to relax. Taking that time away brought stress and thoughts of employees and spending that much money and the reality of the time investment. I think the time was more stressful than the financial investment. Here I am at age 55, and it was going to tie me down for ten years minimum. It is in a remote location; the middle of nowhere. So if anybody was to buy that asset, it was going to be a very unique buyer that wants to buy a brewery outside the metropolitan area.

So how do I get back out of this? I've invested half of our networth into this, how do I get that back out? All those thoughts are going through my mind. I thought, hell, I don't even have a real company yet. I'm about two weeks away from starting to stake out the land for construction. The stress just keeps increasing. Why do I want to go through this? Why am I so driven to do this?"

So, on this time away with Ann and some friends down in Belize, I just woke up one morning and decided, I'm not going to build the brewery. It is not worth the stress that it's putting on me now. And then my mind said, "Oh shit, I've committed to a whole bunch of things and people."

Chapter Six: Rethinking the Startup – Getting Advice

On returning from Belize, instead of notifying the consultants, the project manager, the architects and everybody involved in the project at this point, I just let them know I was busy with other things. They would say, "We need to schedule a meeting." I said, "Yeah, I'm sorry, I'm busy this week and next. We'll put that meeting off." I knew I had my Vistage monthly meeting coming up, and for me, the peer group in Vistage has been so helpful in the fifteen years I've been in there. This would probably be the single largest subject that I've ever brought up to the group.

At that point, the freight train was moving down the tracks. I wasn't sure how to stop it. We were very close to starting to move dirt. Our equipment purchasing list was put together, so we were just about to release a request for quotation package on all the tanks and the brewing equipment. Within thirty days of releasing that, we had to start laying out millions of dollars for equipment. If I was going to stop the train, it was a perfect time to do this.

Often, you walk into the Vistage meeting, and say, "I've got this problem." This one needed a little more thought. I started to compile a Word document. Steve was very good at taking my verbiage, and letting the group know. I'd often say, "Hey, I want to bring this up next week." Steve would lay it out better than I can so I just thought, *Well I'll share this with Steve, and then he can share with the group.* And what ended up happening is Steve shared my entire letter.

I laid out where it started, what had happened in between, and where I was today. I presented that to the group and my commitment to everybody on the team was almost greater than looking in the mirror. I felt such a direct commitment to everybody on that team. As we presented it to the group, of everybody's input, I think Scott W's was the best. And he said, "Patrick, as I recall, within two months of you leaving Steel Inc and Forte, you had started working on this." He said, "Well essentially you've not taken any time off." And as simple as that sounds, I listened to those words from Scott, and I realized he was right. For two months I was so busy wrapping up and going through buckets of money and wills and paperwork and getting my life in order, and having 26 years of my office dumped in the garage. It was going through papers, and, "Do I need this? Do I not need this?" Then I started working on the brewery.

Scott said, "Patrick, if this is such a great idea, would it not also be such a great idea a year from now?" And then Steve chimed in and said, "Look Patrick, you're not going to lose anything." Between Steve and Scott, I realized if this was a good idea today, why would it not be a good idea a year from now? So why not put on the brakes and walk away from it for a little bit, to get some time in between. Then if there was something I still wanted to do in a large form or small form; whether one or ten barrels makes sense, I could come back to it.

That day was so helpful. It was good to have confirmation from my business peers, that it's okay to stop it. That's really what the inner voice was saying, "Stop this." So with that confirmation, I went out to the team members slowly. I approached a few as a group and some individually. I had to move quickly, because I didn't want one group talking to the other group. I didn't tell anybody I might come back and revisit in a year. I didn't want to put up any hopes at all in anybody's mind. I just told them it was over. Somebody along the way said, "Man, you've sure spent a lot of money to get to this point." And I said, "That's okay, I wouldn't trade those days for anything. This was just a great education. I learned so much about an industry I knew nothing about." The things in business are what helped me personally either advise other people or just in my own personal life. I have no regrets over the money spent and the education I've gained over the time.

Right now, it is just two months after our trip to Belize. The more distance between making that decision and now, the better it feels. I can honestly say it was the right thing to shut it down.

I had to decide how to communicate to all the different audiences. Yeah, in a community so small, words spread so fast out here, more so than in the city. I wanted to make sure they heard it from me directly. I tried calling the Mayor out here, and she didn't ever pick up. So I finally sent an email to her, and the rest of city council. I just appreciated their support, and let them know that for personal reasons I have elected not to build the brewery, thank you for your support. I got a reply, "We're saddened; we were looking forward to it." It was short... up to the normal point where she says, "Well we're a growing community, and move onward to development."

I'll be in the rear view mirror very quickly, and people will forget about it. They're sad that they heard the news and the next day they woke up and forgot all about it.

I was blowing up in my mind how difficult the reaction would be from the Mayor, etc. It was a commitment to the community. I don't take commitments lightly in anything. In my mind, I'd committed to the community to build this. It would have been a huge employer in the area. People were already coming up to me and saying, "Sure like to be part of that. I could be on your maintenance crew. I would do this, I could do that." There is that age old phrase that we've all heard that says, "The king is dead: long live the king." Life moves on. And actually what people look at is, "Okay, how does this affect me? I'm sorry he's not going to do that, but now what's the impact on me?" We're all about me, me in this society. And people say, "So, who's the new king going to be?" Or in other words, "What's the new focus?" They move on faster than I think we as business owners think.

We think, "Oh they're going to have a hard time getting over this." The truth is, they just look at what's going to happen to them next.

What Next?

Now the brewery is in the past, I'm looking elsewhere. Time wise and monetarily wise, I've invested a lot out here on the farm. The observation from our farm foreman, Brady, was interesting. It was during the brewery process. We were out here one time and joking, and he said, " I wish you'd go get a job again." I said, "What are you talking about?" He said, "I saw you a lot more when you had Steel Inc, than when you'd been working on this brewery."

It was true. I had, in the year I was working on a brewery, only spent 45 nights here. And I really enjoyed it out here, it's peaceful, it's relaxing.

One other little factor came in. There's an adjoining track of 500 acres of land, and we've been in negotiations on this for over a year. The week before we took off for Belize, we had a signed sales contract. That more than doubles our farm. So the responsibility is to the farm, and that changes some of the aspects. We have enough of our own hay production, and we can increase our grazing capacity as well. We can increase our herd size. Raising cattle's a very interesting business to me. I find it fascinating. Yeah, it's a hobby and probably always will be a hobby. Brady's the brains and the brawn behind this operation. But it's also fun.

I have brought a business aspect into the farming community. We had used old hay cutting equipment. At this point, we've got enough hay leases, where we've leased other people's property to make hay. We really needed to speed that up, because it would be every farm hand on deck. Brady's dad was helping. We'd have cutters, we'd have hay rakes, we'd have balers to get this done. I said, "We need to get more modern cutting equipment that moves faster." Brady called me back, and said, "Okay, they're on sale." This was in May. The hay cutting equipment's on sale. Perfect time to call. And I said, "Brady, we're coming into hay season, why would a manufacturer put a sale on one of the number one prime time items?" "I don't know." I said, "Well go ask." So he called back, and said, "Well the reason that one's on sale is because they've come up with a brand new model; the first model change in over ten years." And I said, "Well Brady, how much more is that?" "Well it's another $5000 more than the old style." That one piece of equipment eliminates one entire tractor and one entire man hour. We can cut more than twice the amount of hay with that piece of equipment. Now, my only point is, it was fun to take a business mindset to analyze why I would have paid that on sale and said, "Wow, let's buy it because it's on sale." Bring the business aspect to the farm, and we've increased our hay production with buying a few new pieces of equipment that operate more efficiently than we did before. That can't happen every day out here, but the farm will see more of me, or I'll see more of the farm. It'll be one of those things. I truly still have a little housekeeping to do with the windfall of cash from Steel Inc. Those boxes are still in the garage—26 years of Steel Inc.

Packing Away Steel Inc

It's 26 years—you just can't throw 'em out. I haven't put the time into it, so that's one of the things I'm going to be working on. I can't throw it out now. I'm not going back to the steel business. Yet, it was difficult to take a piece of paper or whatever it was and throw it out. Say it's a reference chart that I used almost every day in the steel business. Well hell, I don't need it now. Between the farm, some travel with Ann, and cleaning that up I'll be busy enough.

The Rodeo

Ann said, "You're not happy unless you have a project going." And that means building something. One of the things we had bought is a type of horse called the reining horse. These horses were trained in arenas. I didn't want to use them in an arena, but I understood the arena, because sometimes when they get in the pasture too long, they forget their training. If you create an arena, it's confined and you can get that horse back into sync. So I wanted to have that arena. I didn't just go slap it up. I started interviewing people, and said, "Hey I see you've got an arena, why is yours all steel? Why is yours all wood? Why did you pick this size? Why did you pick that size?" It was one way to just understand people's design structure.

I ended up with a combination of steel and wood for various reasons. We were going to put it across a creek, which would be maybe half to a mile away. Then we thought, why do that? Would you really use it as much if it wasn't convenient? Then we started looking at locations and picked this location over here. We construct the arena and a holding area for cattle to work in training with the horse.

I said, "Brady let's just put some two by sixes across the top of this gate. Then we could have a little deck where we drink beer and have a look down at the other people riding." He said, "Man, it's going to be hot up there, why don't we get a roof over it as well?" So we built a platform with a roof, and then Mike, one of Brady's best friends who has worked here at the farm also, said, "Hell you're getting all this out here, why don't you just have your own rodeo?"

There was a seed planted. We started talking about it. What's the reality of having some cowboys out here, just doing a little fun thing? So we did it in year one. We had eight cowboys and on purpose, Ann and I invited almost nobody from Houston but the kids and whatever friends they wanted. We really wanted this to be a community event, and to get to know our neighbors and people of the community. We had just the Houston folks who lived on the road. They were invited and other neighbors up here. It was a hit. It was a hit with the cowboys, too.

At Steel Inc, we did a lot of large dinners and things for the company, but also we did a turkey day, the day before

Thanksgiving. That was a party for 500, so this was nothing to me. I mean some people say, "Oh my goodness, how did you do that?" We've been doing this for years. A lot of what I learned there, I could bring up here. So we had a rodeo, and then we had a barbecue catered. We had a band, and inside we had a true barn dance. Year one came off well, and the community loved it.

Year two comes, and we thought, well we'd better add this grandstand a little bit to create some shade, and we'll put up some tents. And even more people came. And so then we created an event, and there's even more. That year, people said, "I can't hear the announcer anymore." This year we put in a complete PA system. Now everybody can hear music, along with the PA announcer. We've got the same guy doing the announcing. He knows all the cowboys, so he can tell a little side story and be funny, and he's just a natural with a microphone. We keep times, and we do something unique. All these cowboys know each other, but till the day they show up they don't know who their working partner's going to be. We draw names out of a hat, and they find out that moment who their partner is. So they can't pre-plan and work and strategize ahead of time. That's how real rodeos are; you're used to working together with somebody, and so it's interesting to see how they have to work together instantly. Last year we brought kids' events into it. That was even a bigger hit. So this year we focused on kids' events. We did more and had three cowboy events, and also went too long last year. We shortened it this year, and included both cowboy events and kid's events. Time, that's it, let's go have a beer. And again, I can't tell you how many people came up to me and thanked me for doing this.

Why do I do this? I don't know that I can answer other than saying, "I enjoy being part of the community out here, and it's kind of a way to give back." There have been so many people who've been so kind to me and my family as we were outsiders coming in. It's a way to say, "Thanks and I appreciate your friendship."

Food

What intrigues me is where our food source comes from. Brady and I knew nothing about gardening. He knew his grandma had one, and I've never grown one. We came out here, and we created a garden, and it was plentiful. We had so many vegetables! The first year we just stumbled through it, but now the garden's become a real focus for me. I think this is one of the things I want to learn even more about. That will be maintaining that garden and doing it even better than we've done it. Along with the garden is a meat processing building. I started to draw this, and the brewery got in the way and I put it on hold, but I've already got an appointment with the architect.

This structure I'm working on has various functions. I want to be able to have a slaughter chute. You bring a cow in, and kill it, and then you hang it up, skin it, and gut it. Then you roll it into a cooler to chill the meat. That cooler opens up into this new building. And in the new building we will be able to process that beef. We'll be able to saw it, cut it, package it, and freeze it. We can do that with any animal; hogs, deer, cattle. Cattle are the biggest, and that's what we're designing around. The building does other things too. We've started canning. Ann and I canned tomato sauce the other night. We've canned pickles, we've canned squash. We're learning, and last year I did both freezing and canning of green beans.

The building will have multiple pieces of equipment for processing convenience. This place will be set up as a sanitary, stainless steel kitchen. All the canning equipment will be right there. So all I need to do is take the vegetables there, wash 'em, can 'em, preserve 'em. We'll have meat processing equipment too. We have meat grinders and sausage stuffers. One day in the barn, we bought some hog meat, Brady had some too, and then we had some deer meat. We got together with some neighbors down the road, Brady and his mom and dad. And we're just out there drinking beer and having a good time. We made over 200 pounds of sausage on a cool February day.

Also inside this building, there's small brewing equipment. This could actually become a food processing facility, so we'll be able to make beer in a clean, sterile environment. We'll be able to process animals, and also vegetables. By the way, this food processing is a hobby, because we're not doing it for resale. Having capital to be able to throw at something like this is useful. It's a huge education. I'm learning, studying the equipment and it's fascinating in itself.

Another thing we're doing is growing hops out here, and this is fully experimental. We've got five different varieties and we have real estate to grow that on. If this takes off as a test, and we find some varieties that take off, I think that could be a business. To be able to sell Texas hops to Texas brewers would be huge. People would put on the label, "Made with Texas hops." So even though it's an experiment, there is a business aspect to that. Again, with the real estate, we can grow it. We could make that a business.

Chapter Seven: Perspective from Ann on the Journey

Ann is Patrick's wife. This chapter describes the story during and after the Steel Inc sale from her perspective.

Did we ever think about separating from Simon before the sale? Patrick and a couple of other salesmen were going to try to buy out Simon about fifteen years ago. It just didn't happen for a lot of reasons. I think Patrick realized that wasn't the fair way of doing it, and it wasn't the right time. He just took on more responsibility I think, and Simon left him alone to do that. So that was fine.

It came up again maybe ten years before the sale to Forte, because things were difficult. When that didn't go through, I think then Patrick decided he should've worked it out another way. He took over more of the responsibilities and that made it easier for him.

Then as the company grew larger, and he couldn't oversee everything, he started letting go of things. Some key employees started bucking him too. That's when I think he started considering the company had become too big, bigger than he wanted to handle. It wasn't the same company. We would go to the Christmas parties, and I would have to have him go over all the employees and their names. He had to stop and think about names, and I didn't know many of the employees. It started taking on different dynamics within the company.

A couple of days a week, Patrick used to call and say, "I'm headed home now." An hour later, he would leave, and he'd say, "Oh Ann, I'm so sorry. So and so came up, and they had a problem with their daughter," Or, "They have a problem with money," or, "The car broke down and they want to talk to me about it." For a while, I think he was bound up with people and their lives. That's just part of who he is. Then it got to the point when it was so big that he didn't know people as well. It wasn't the small, personal company that he was used to. I think that's when he started thinking, it may be the time to sell.

The other factor is he wanted to grow the company internationally. At that point in our lives we thought, how much more of our money do we want to risk? He was really excited to grow it. Maybe bringing in outside capital was the way to expand. Then he did get some interest, and that idea went on for a couple of years.

Then he got cancer. At that point, he really took a hard look at our whole future and the future of the business. Also, our boys were growing up. Collin had worked for the company in the summers. Patrick realized that working for the company was not what our boys wanted to do in the future. That was a pretty big turning point for us.

We did not want them to be partners with Simon's kids. That's unfair to them, and from a mother's perspective, I definitely didn't want that. Also, I told Patrick, "It took you fifteen years to grow the company. You started with very little. To expect our boys to come in at 25 or 30 or even 35 is highly unfair because you've built this huge company that would be hard for them to step into. They don't have the knowledge and the experience. Patrick once said, "If I would've known how hard it was to start a company, I would have never done it." He said, "I was young and stupid, we were young and risk takers."

Why should we expect our boys to (a) want to do this and (b) to be able to do it? So how much longer would we want to wait before we turned it over? They weren't all that interested. Collin might have been, Jack might have been at some point, but they just weren't committed; it wasn't their journey. Between that and the cancer, we finally just said, "Enough's enough. It's grown too big."

We had plans of Patrick working for a public company, and continuing to travel. We thought the headaches of owning the company would be gone, and they would let Patrick expand the company. But that just didn't take place.

In terms of rethinking our future there were two or three times before when he considered selling. It drove me a little crazy because it was this constant, "I'm going to sell. No I'm not. I'm going to sell it. I'm not." That part was difficult. Once he crossed that line and made his decision, people tried to talk him out of it. It was, "Why are you doing this?" But he crossed the line. I saw it happen. He said, "No, this is my direction, I'm going to sell." So it went forward.

There were very difficult negotiations that went on with the sale and we weren't too sure it would go through. I think once he made up his mind, it was done. We've ridden the highs and lows in the oil industry. When we knew we were at a high, we knew that if we didn't sell now, we might have to wait eight or ten years to do it. That was too long. The opportunity was there.

What was the actual feeling once the sale was made? Patrick grew the business and there came a time where financially we were comfortable. It had been very good to us. I've always thought of all the years that he didn't get home until 8:15 at night, and the boys didn't see him. I was holding down the fort, and life wasn't easy. I always had this vision, "Oh when he sells the company, I'm going to buy myself a brand new car." Or, "We're going to do this, we're going to do that." It was more of a relief that we'd crossed the line. It wasn't "Oh my Gosh, I've got money to spend." It was more of an emotional windfall for me "Okay, I can relax now." Then we had to make some tough decisions, and we were making those tough decisions while he was going through his treatments. We began working with financial advisors and lawyers to get our house in order.

In some ways, I came to it from a different perspective. My feeling at the time was one of fear. "What if something did happen to him? I've got to start paying attention more and know what's going on." We were very fortunate to have some good advisers with us.

Tom was probably my favorite. We were in a meeting with a lawyer, and I felt almost assaulted, with questions coming at me. And at one point, he looked at me and just said, "Do we need to stop?" I said, "Yes." It was nice to have someone else looking after me too. I didn't want our life to really change. If anything, I wanted our life to become more private. We had always tried to keep it pretty private. I didn't want my boys to be affected. That was, I guess my biggest thought. It came at a pretty critical time in their lives. They were figuring out their career paths. They don't want for anything but it doesn't mean that it's a given that they get whatever they want. They have both worked and understand the value of a dollar. I've always told them, responsibility comes with having money.

At some point both boys, had indicated to us, "you need to go on this cruise," or, "You need to do this," or, "You need to take Mom here." Patrick came home one day and said, "All of a sudden, I'm getting dating advice from my boys." So they wanted us to enjoy our time. They knew life had been hectic and busy. There'd been other illnesses in the family, and a lot going on outside of our immediate family, that had taken up a lot of my time. It was nice to see them be the ones to push us to enjoy ourselves a little bit.

The news did of course become public and we started to receive a number of calls for donations. We had a few other business people we knew call and ask for money. Wealth advisers, and insurance people still call. Luckily, we'd had those people in place a long time ago. Even when there wasn't much money we've had advisors in place. So that helps. It was really easier to say, "No thank you, we have someone we've dealt with for fifteen years." It's a little disappointing I guess, that people come out of the woodwork and want to borrow money or want money from you. But I think you have to take it from their perspective. They're just trying to do their job and trying to make ends meet. They're trying for all they can get. So, I give them credit for going for it and asking. You just learn to say, "No, I can't help you." And you find the places that you are passionate aout & where your money will make a difference.

In terms of family calling, they didn't. I know you can go online and you can find out all the details, but I don't know if anyone really did. I guess some people don't even realize or know, and that's just how we've kept it. Even before the sale, we've been very blessed to help when there were family members or people in need. There's nothing like the financial means and the time to help others. I can't imagine families that have no one to go to for any sort of help; emotional, financial or physical.

The corporate world was fascinating. I looked forward every day to Patrick coming home from work and telling me all about it. It was a world we had never been exposed to. He was at a corporate level that was totally foreign to us. Just the way they did business was foreign to us. There were some wonderful conversations, and a lot of learning going on. We really had hoped that would continue, because it was exciting. It was a way of doing business to learn about.

Regarding the corporate world and things changing, it didn't take long. Patrick's always been able to say what he wants to say and make decisions when he wants to make decisions. When you have to have a meeting every day just to discuss everything, and be careful what you say, it was getting pretty evident it wasn't going to work. They really didn't want his opinion. It was a part of the corporate world of, "Well I know better." It was interesting. It was sad. Nobody wanted to listen; they wanted to talk about themselves. It was all about them. What their past accomplishments were at another job, or from a long time ago. It wasn't much about, "What are you doing now, and where are you going to go now?" It was a very "me me me" environment. We saw pretty quickly that there was not much cooperation. They were stopping the way of doing business that had made Steel Inc. successful and preventing them from moving forward. The reaction time was so flawed and slow. Patrick expected that. He didn't expect they wouldn't be willing to even attempt to listen. The employees were suffering.

Patrick couldn't make things the way they wanted it to be. They wanted it to be the same as before the sale and no one wanted to change. That was sad to see for the employees.

Patrick decided to leave, and we were now talking about what he would do with his time. Patrick enjoys trying different beers.

The craft brewing business is doing well and that sounded like a great idea. We toured several places. It was fun. We got to travel and talk to the people. Everyone we talked to was passionate; they loved what they're doing and they were hands on. I think that's what drew us to it. He could get back to something very hands on, and that was his interest. Everyone that you talked to just loved their job. They could be losing money, and they were just so happy.

What I had thought would be a small undertaking soon got a life of its own. Patrick started talking to consultants. He'd go with the consultants to see people in the community. He had meetings with advertising agencies, architects, and distributors. This was, "Hey let's play, this is really fun, it's cool." I think it snowballed into this wonderful fantasy project. I thought it was just getting way too big.

I think he considered it a business rather than a hobby. It wasn't a business in the sense that it had to support our retirement and our future. It was a business of passion, and we could provide some jobs for a community. Patrick's very project-oriented and always likes to have something going on. This was another project, another challenge, for him. Once he accomplishes this he'llgo on to the next project.

Patrick did not know anything about the consumer business. I think the learning curve was his carrot. Just to learn something new and to be excited by something new. He started spending less and less time at the farm, because he had meetings all during the week. Then about five months ago, he was getting up in the middle of the night to work just like he used to do. He was getting up at two or three in the morning and working for an hour or two and coming back to bed. It was the same habits that he'd had before. I think that's when he realized that this is going to be too much. I just left this; I don't want to go back. With Patrick, when he asks for my opinion or my gut feeling, I can give it to him. But when he's not ready to hear it, he's not ready to hear it. I watched him over the course of several months get to the realization that this is just getting too big and too much work. I saw the train coming before he did. I wasn't going to say anything until he realized it, because I didn't want him to think that he didn't get to work through his decision. At some point he'll find something else. Whether it's beer on a small scale or helping someone else as a consultant. I don't know what he'll do, but he'll do something.

He was obviously feeling pressured. Then we were on vacation, and he had some distance from the project. That's when he said, "I'm getting into a full time job again, and that was not my intention." I think it was hard. I think he'd say, "I wouldn't take it back. All the time, money, energy and learning something new was worth it." I'm sure he's disappointed in a way, but I think he knows that it was just too much.

Patrick had described that on the planning side, this was getting to be a really big financial commitment. We were talking about some millions of dollars. I wasn't happy about it. I'm the conservative one in the family. I'm the one that's worried about having enough money to live on for the rest of our lives. He always tells me to stop worrying. Most of our expences were Farm expenses. And the Farm is what Patrick really enjoys. That's his de-stressor. I want that to continue to be something that's his. I look at farm spending almost as play money. If that's what gives him pleasure, and I enjoy it too, then that's where we need to be spending our money.

Patrick was spending more time at the farm and doing some really enjoyable things for the community He built a horse arena complete with stands and started to have a July 4th rodeo with volunteer cowboys, prizes, music and food. The community loved it. So when you ask me now about spending time and money at the farm; is that a hobby or a business? I would say more a hobby. It does not need to create income. Do I want the farm to have the cattle business start making money? Yes... or at least to break even. I don't want to keep propping it up. But if all it does is break even and lose a little money here and there, and he's happy and we're happy then there's a hobby and that's fine. Really if you think about it, it's a hobby to build a strong future value. It can be sold off if we want to. The value of ranch property has continued to go up. On paper it looks good.

The boys thought the beer business idea was fun. "Wouldn't it be cool to say, I'm Vice President or a President of a brewery." I think the boys also understood the financial commitment and the work it was going to take. If their dad decided it was too much, then it was truly too much. They know Patrick, and they know how hard he can work, and how much time and energy he can put into something. Patrick will give 200% into everything he does.

When the kids were pre-teen I was going crazy at both ends. I was resentful at times of Patrick's time at work, and time away from the kids and me. I was really busy. Then it hit me " Patrick does everything 200% or nothing. If he works 200%, if he plays 200%, if he loves his kids 200%, I can't take that away from him. I can't say, "Well you can only work 100% and you have to love us 200%, and you have to change." That's not possible." I just accepted that he does things that way, and learned to be happy for it. I can't take that away from him, because then he's not who he is. Then I don't get loved 200%, and the boys don't get loved 200%. Don't try to change him; you can't.

So now we have come full circle, and I sometimes think what will happen next? I don't know. I honestly think it's going to be a little unsettling for a couple of years until he finds a groove that he wants to get into. I feel for him, because I think he's going to struggle with that. I can't pick something for him or fix that for him; nobody can. I guess I'm just going to be prepared to let him come up with some ideas and see them through. I hope they're on a much smaller scale, and I think he's learned that. But he will drive me crazy if he's around the house all the time, wanting to follow me around. My day is my day, and I do my thing. Then when he's at home, we sit down and have dinner in the house, just like always. He's been real respectful of my time as far as that goes. I believe you sell your business when you believe the time is right. I think there's that gut instinct. You can totally get there, but once you get there, I think you just move forward and you don't look back. Maybe jumping into the brewery was too much; he should've taken some time. I think that's what I would tell people; "Move forward with your plans, but take some time." There's a lot to clean up after a sale, money and details to arrange and structure. A lot of decisions have to be made and a lot of paperwork has to be done. That part of it is not fun, and it's exhausting. Maybe it's not what I expected. That's why it was difficult. My advice is, don't ever rush that, but take it slow. Take it in small snippets, then take several weeks off and enjoy yourself. Then come back to it. That's what I wish we could have done. Again, it was the cancer situation that I think made Patrick feel so responsible in getting to "We've got to get it done." I appreciate that, because we really did have to get it done.

Chapter Eight: Conclusion and Insights about Patrick's Story

After the sale the CEO is sometimes involved on an ongoing basis with the new owner. This is what happened with Patrick. Often, as demonstrated, this will not last very long. The real exit happens after the person leaves the new purchasing company.

From talking with several different CEO clients of mine this is the time. When the real exit begins, periods of anxiety and even depression may set in for these who have been extremely busy people with many meetings, phone calls, and emails.

The anxiety and loneliness then begins to set in because all of a sudden the phone calls stop, the meetings stop, and they may receive very few emails. This becomes a real threat to their egos. They wonder how important they are, and what significance they have. What will take up their time now in the future?

One observation from Patrick's case is to recognize that they have some urgency to start to think about what activity will start to fill their life. Often they want to come to that conclusion rather quickly.

I think this is a mistake; they actually are not ready yet to make that decision. Time is needed to reflect, to decompress from the prior super busy life of the CEO. When they decide to start something maybe a new business, I have found there is an important question to ask.

Is this a hobby or a business? It can be either. But depending on the choice, a very different approach will be necessary.

It is a difficult question to answer as the ego may get in the way and it may be hard for someone to say it is a hobby! I believe this difficulty happened with Patrick. I believe he wanted it to be a hobby...But he responded as if it was a business. This drove an approach with some very high spending assumptions.

The CEO Personality

As we saw in the sequence of Patrick's journey, the CEO personality does not do very well at just stepping back and reflecting for lengthy time periods. The life reflection is over the question "so what comes next?"

How do you determine this passion? It is hard to just determine while staring at a blank sheet of paper. The aha moment in Patrick's story was the conversation about what he had been actually doing with his time at the farm, over the last few years. This was more a *discovery* process than merely determining your passion. Look at your activities, your events in your spare time and you may *discover* this passion. I think Patrick found this in the idea of food preparation for the rodeo events for the community. He may develop the Brand...Sandy Creek Ranch Products. It will most likely be a hobby but who knows...someday a gradual business could emerge, on its own and organically. This is a valuable process.

Who is Steve Brody?

Let's back up a little and provide some context to this whole story. Who am I and what is my relationship with these CEOs?

I am Steve Brody, a Chair for Vistage International, the world's largest CEO member organization. As of July 2015 we have almost 20,000 members in the US plus about twelve other countries. My role is one of Executive Coach and advisor to these Execs. I am one of thirteen Chairs in Houston and one of about 500 Chairs in the US. None of the Chairs are employees. We are Independent Contractors. The parent firm is privately owned, based in San Diego, and does over $100 MM Revenue with about 150 employees. Growth is generated by adding more Chairs in many markets in the country. In almost every major market we operate CEO peer groups. A group is made up of twelve to sixteen firms that do not compete with each other, are mostly privately held and have a revenue of between $5mm to $500mm per year. We call this the middle market.

The mission overall is to: Increase the effectiveness and enhance the lives of CEOs.

This is a highly purpose driven mission that appeals to certain people as Chairs and members. It is not for everyone; primarily for people who believe in lifelong learning and development and who want to emphasize self-improvement and growth.

Meetings are scheduled monthly for a full day including a workshop with an expert resource speaker. They also include an Executive session where members raise strategic topics for advice and input from their peers. Also each month there is a private Coaching meeting with the Chair to focus on key priorities for the CEO and the firm. These are not casual meetings or conversations. They are probing, in-depth, challenging, and stimulating to drive better leadership habits, management, and accountability.

Chairs tend to have a deep and experienced background from any industry and are driven by helping others to generate success. Twenty to thirty years of business experience is customary and you can think of this work as a "calling or higher purpose". Depending on how many Groups the Chair is leading, they will be doing other work or consulting outside of Vistage.

What was my path to becoming a Chair? It included sixteen years with a Division of the Coca-Cola Company leaving as Sen VP Marketing for the Minute Maid Co. I had ten years as President of four different consumer firms all owned by Investors or Equity Groups. Now I have had sixteen years as a Chair in Houston.

The Chairs are all fascinating people, very eclectic and intellectually stimulating! It actually is a tribe and a close group of peers. Vistage is the leader in this field and has spawned a variety of smaller competitors.

Reflecting Patrick's Story

Patrick's entire story reflects a trend that can be predicted with business owners, CEOs that will be considering or in the process of exiting or transitioning from their business. By some estimates there will be 5mm firms that will be sold within the next ten years in the US. These conditions will be happening over and over again.

I have already started to witness this trend with several of my CEO clients over the last several years. It is a demographic trend that is growing. After it happens they tend to leave their Vistage Group, not always but most of the time. Based on this trend I have started a new Peer Advisory Group and have affiliated with a retired Canadian Chair. The concept is called NAVIOND which means, Navigating life after business and beyond. Description at www.Naviond.com.

This audience can be described as

Folks who are 50 +
Financially independent
Sold or retired from their firms
Not involved with day to day management anymore. They are now in the second half of their lives. They are active and curious people, who are moving from success to significance A Peer Advisory Group is interesting for them but not on a monthly basis. They want to deal with more personal or family ideas or how they can help others and devote time to causes or events that stimulate them. Topics covered in these meetings include:

Having family discussions about their wealth, legacy, estates, desires
Review investments, portfolio management
What is their current passion business, charitable, hobbies, other
What they do for fun
How to maintain and improve health
Religious and spiritual focus...How to improve the world

www.ingramcontent.com/pod-product-compliance
Lightning Source LLC
Chambersburg PA
CBHW071610170526
45166CB00003B/1044